D1271597

BUILDING BLOCKS OF MATTER

MIXTURES AND SOLUTIONS

Louise and Richard Spilsbury

Heinemann Library
Chicago, Illinois

Designed by Richard Parker and Tinstar Design Ltd, www.tinstar.co.uk
Printed and bound in China by Leo Paper Group

11 10 09 08 07
10 9 8 7 6 5 4 3 2 1

Library of Congress Cataloging-in-Publication Data
Spilsbury, Louise.
  Mixtures and solutions / Louise and Richard Spilsbury.
    p. cm. -- (Building blocks of matter)
  Includes bibliographical references and index.
  ISBN-13: 978-1-4034-9339-2 (lib. bdg.)
  ISBN-10: 1-4034-9339-1 (lib. bdg.)
  ISBN-13: 978-1-4034-9344-6 (pbk.)
  ISBN-10: 1-4034-9344-8 (pbk.)
  1. Solutions (Chemistry)--Juvenile literature. 2. Mixtures--Juvenile literature. 3. Matter--Properties--Juvenile literature. I. Spilsbury, Richard, 1963- II. Title.
  QD541.S69 2007
  541'.34--dc22
                          2006025746

Acknowledgments
The publishers would like to thank the following for permission to reproduce photographs: Alamy p. 13 (Phil Degginger); Corbis pp. 6 (Ashley Cooper), 20 (Michael S. Yamashita), 5 (Zefa/José Fuste Raga); Digital Stock p. 4; Getty Images pp. 10 (AFP), 10 (Iconica/Nichola Evans), 28 (Image Bank/Wayne Levin), 25 (Photographer's Choice/Hugh Sitton), 14 (Stone/Ken Whitmore); Harcourt Education (Tudor Photography) pp. 9, 11 top & bottom, 15, 16, 18 top & bottom, 19, 21, 24 top & bottom, 27; Masterfile p. 26 (Garry Black); NHPA p. 17 (Joe Blossom); Photolibrary.com pp. 12 (Foodpix/Judd Pilossof), 23 (Robert Harding Picture Library/Bruno Barbier).

Cover photograph of delicate patterns forming in colored water reproduced with permission of Masterfile (J. A. Kraulis).

Every effort has been made to contact copyright holders of any material reproduced in this book. Any omissions will be rectified in subsequent printings if notice is given to the publishers.

The publishers would like to thank Nick Sample for his help with the preparation of this book.

Disclaimer
All the Internet addresses (URLs) given in this book were valid at the time of going to press. However, due to the dynamic nature of the Internet, some addresses may have changed, or sites may have changed or ceased to exist since publication. While the author and publishers regret any inconvenience this may cause readers, no responsibility for any such changes can be accepted by either the author or the publishers.

Contents

Any words appearing in the text in bold, **like this**, are explained in the Glossary.

What Are Mixtures and Solutions?

Everything in the world is made up of **matter**. All matter, even air, occupies space and has **mass**. Matter is made from tiny building blocks called **atoms**. Some matter is made up of just one type of atom. Most matter is made from groups of different atoms joined together called **molecules**.

There are many different types of matter. They all have different **physical properties**—for example, color, hardness, smell, or shape. They also have different **chemical properties**. These describe how atoms behave when they are mixed with other types of atom.

Together or joined up?

When we mix different types of matter, sometimes they form a mixture. The matter gets mixed up, but each type keeps its chemical properties. Other times, the matter combines to form a new substance called a **compound**. A compound has different physical and chemical properties than the materials that formed it.

When we mix different coins together, they do not change properties. They can be separated again, just like a mixture can.

How are solutions and mixtures different?

Solutions are a type of mixture. In solutions, atoms or molecules get mixed together so much that they cannot be separated as easily as in other mixtures. We say one substance **dissolves** into another. For example, a fizzy cola drink is made when sugary cola syrup and carbon dioxide **gas** dissolve in water. Molecules of cola and carbon dioxide become evenly spread among the water molecules.

Did you know?
Not a solution

A mixture such as sand and water does not form a solution. When we mix sand and water together, we can see the sand spaced evenly in the water. This is called a **suspension**. But when we stop mixing, the suspension changes. Sand starts to fall or settle to the bottom of the mixing container. The sand and the water separate.

The colored dye we use to change the color of cloth is a type of solution.

5

Mixed states

One way we describe matter is by its **state**. The three states of matter are **solid**, **liquid,** and gas. In solids, strong forces hold atoms or molecules tightly together. In liquids and gases, these forces are weaker. This means the atoms or molecules are further apart and can move past each other.

Mixtures and solutions can be any combination of states. For example, a puddle of muddy water contains solid **particles** of soil mixed in liquid water.

Tiny particles of solids mixed with gases form smoke in the air.

Did you know?
Changing state

Soil is a mixture. It contains tiny bits of solids including rock, dead plants and animals, and waste. It also contains water and air. Soil is continuously mixed together by underground animals such as insects, worms, and moles and also by growing plant roots. Soils in different places look different because they are a mix of different rocks and other types of matter.

How substances dissolve

To make any solution, there has to be a **solute** and a **solvent**. The solute is the substance that dissolves. The solvent is the substance doing the dissolving. For example, in salt water, water is the solvent and salt is the solute. A solution forms as each molecule of solute is separated from the other molecules of solute. This happens when the solvent atoms or molecules fill the gaps between them.

Salt is made of crystals. Each crystal contains sodium and chlorine atoms held closely together. When salt dissolves in water, the water molecules start to tug at the sodium and chlorine atoms on the outside of the crystals. Soon the pull from water molecules becomes greater than the force holding the sodium and chlorine atoms together. The atoms leave the crystal. Gradually each sodium and chlorine atom is separated and spread out by the water molecules.

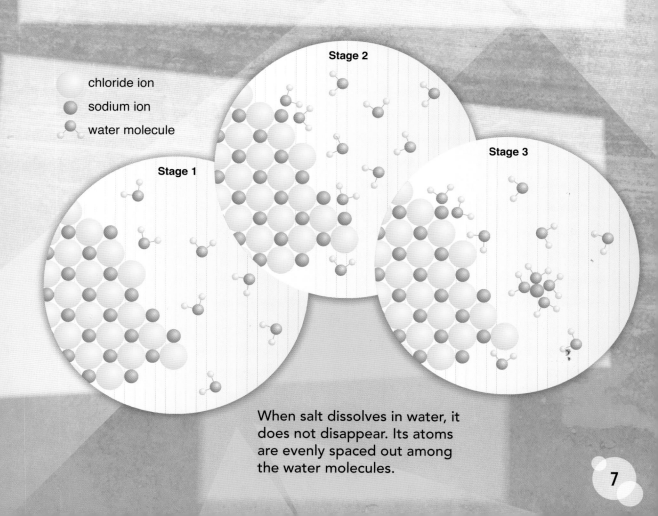

chloride ion

sodium ion

water molecule

Stage 1

Stage 2

Stage 3

When salt dissolves in water, it does not disappear. Its atoms are evenly spaced out among the water molecules.

Types of solvent

Most solvents are liquids, and water is the most common solvent. However, there are some substances that do not dissolve in water. For example, oil is **insoluble** in water. However, oil can dissolve in other solvents such as kerosene. Kerosene is a liquid with molecules similar to those in oil.

Did you know?
Metal solvents

Some solids such as iron can be used as solvents! Pure iron only contains iron atoms. It is a strong metal, but it is brittle. People make tougher steel by melting iron at high temperatures until it is liquid and then dissolving carbon in it. When the solution cools, it hardens, with the carbon atoms spread evenly among the iron atoms. Metal solutions such as steel are called alloys.

This black oil forms a sticky trail in the water because it does not dissolve.

How Do We Measure Mixtures and Solutions?

We often measure substances by **mass** or **volume**. Mass is the amount of **matter** a substance contains. Its volume is the amount of space it takes up. In a mixture, the total mass is equal to the sum of the masses of each substance. However, we can also measure **solutions** in other ways.

Concentration and strength

Concentration is the mass or volume of **solute** in a given volume of solution. For example, the concentration of a sugar solution could be 0.35 ounces (10 grams) of sugar for each liter of water. We can also describe concentration as parts per million. For example, there are about 35,000 **molecules** of salt to every million molecules of water in seawater.

A solution with a high concentration of solute is said to be strong. A less concentrated solution is said to be more **diluted**. This means there are more **solvent particles** around each bit of solute.

The jar on the left contains tap water. In the jar on the right, salt has been dissolved into the water. The total volume and total mass have increased.

9

Watercolor painters can add more or less water to paint solutions. This makes the color darker or lighter.

Did you know?
Color and taste

Color and taste are used to compare the concentration of some solutions. For example, orange juice gets lighter in color and weaker in taste when diluted. Scientists sometimes use machines to compare solutions by color. However, they rarely use taste, since many substances are unsafe to drink!

Ease of dissolving

If you stir more and more salt into a glass of water, eventually some salt will not **dissolve**. It piles up in the glass. When this happens, we say the solution is **saturated**. **Solubility** is a measure of how much solute will dissolve in a solvent before the solution becomes saturated. For example, only a small amount of lead chloride will dissolve in a liter of water. Much more zinc chloride will dissolve before the solution is saturated. We say that zinc chloride's solubility is greater.

Experiment
Concentrated sugar

Problem: Why can't I dissolve any more sugar?

Hypothesis: When the solution is saturated, no more sugar will dissolve.

You will need:
- a wide glass
- a teaspoon
- granulated sugar
- a pen and paper

Procedure:
1 Half-fill the glass with warm water and place it on a table.
2 Add one teaspoon of sugar to the water. Stir until it dissolves (it will disappear). Mark "number of spoons" on the paper and write one check mark (✓) underneath.
3 Repeat step 2 until the sugar does not disappear.

Results: How many spoons of sugar did the water dissolve?

Conclusion: When sugar dissolves, each sugar molecule is surrounded by water molecules. A water molecule that is linked to one sugar molecule cannot link to another. As more sugar dissolves, the free water molecules are used up. Eventually no more sugar can dissolve. It collects at the bottom of the glass.

How Do We Make Mixtures?

Some mixtures are made just by stirring substances together. Others are made by breaking down the substances into smaller pieces. People use tools such as knives, saws, blenders, grinders, and graters to break up **matter**. This is only a **physical change**. For example, fruit in a blender turns from fruit-shaped matter into colorful mush.

Suspensions

In a **solution**, the **solute's atoms** or **molecules** stay evenly spread out. A **suspension** is a mixture in which atoms or molecules are spread out but do not **dissolve**. For example, when we mix oil and water together, the oil breaks into tiny droplets among the water molecules. When the suspension is left still, the oil droplets bunch together and form a separate layer on top of the water.

A fruit's flavor is one of its **physical properties**. A smoothie's flavor is a mix of the flavors of the individual fruits.

Longer lasting mixtures

Density is the amount of **mass** in a certain **volume** of a substance. For example, a block of lead is heavier than a block of wood of the same size. This is because the lead block has more, heavier atoms packed together in each bit of its volume than the wood. We say that lead has a greater density than wood.

Suspensions will separate if the substances in them have different densities. If we make the densities similar, the suspension will last longer. For example, toothpaste is a mixture of **solids** and water. Toothpaste makers add thickeners such as seaweed to the mix. This gives water a density similar to that of the solids. The mixture will not separate, and each squeeze of the tube will give the same combination of ingredients.

Salad dressing made from oil and vinegar quickly separates. Store-bought dressing stays mixed for longer. Added thickeners make the densities of the oil and vinegar solutions similar.

CASE STUDY:
The right shade

Mixing blue and yellow paint makes green paint. However, there are lots of different shades of green. Stores that sell house paints create the colors that customers want. They use color-mixing machines to make sure that each color is the same whenever it is made.

The store worker first chooses a base color. This is dense, grayish paint. A light final color, such as sky blue, needs a lighter base color than a dark final color. The worker then types a code for the chosen color into the machine. This tells the machine what paint recipe to use. The machine squirts exact amounts from separate containers into an open can of the base color. The can is closed tightly before the machine shakes the paint very fast to mix the color molecules evenly. The paint formed is a long-lasting suspension.

Paint machines produce exactly the right shade and make sure that all the paint in a can is the same color.

14

What Makes Dissolving Easier?

Solutions form when a **solute** is added to a **solvent**. They usually form faster when the solvent bumps into the solute faster and more often. There are several ways that we can make solutes **dissolve** more easily.

Heat

Atoms or **molecules** are always **vibrating** (shaking around). Heat is a form of energy. When we heat a substance, its atoms or molecules vibrate faster. This is because the extra energy loosens the force holding the atoms or molecules together.

A hot solvent bumps faster into solute atoms or molecules. It also pulls on them harder. A hot solute breaks up more easily, so solvent atoms or molecules can surround the bits of solute more rapidly. This means that heat increases the **solubility** of many substances. For example, just-boiled water can dissolve a third more sugar than just-melted ice water.

An instant drink powder is a solute. It will dissolve more easily in hot water.

Did you know?
Losing fizz

A warm glass of fizzy soda has fewer bubbles than a cold one. Unlike **liquids** and **solids**, a **gas** becomes less soluble when it is heated. The heat energy makes gas molecules move so fast that they bunch together in bubbles. These rise through the liquid because they are less **dense** than it is. When carbon dioxide bubbles come out of the soda solution, they leave the drink tasting flat.

Stirring and pressure

If you kick a ball hard, it moves faster than if you kick it gently. The push on a certain area of an object is called **pressure**. Pressure can increase the energy of atoms or molecules. One way of pushing solvent and solute atoms or molecules together is by stirring. Stirring brings new molecules of the solvent into contact with the solute. This speeds up dissolving.

Stirring a stock cube pushes its molecules against water molecules and makes it dissolve more easily.

Solute size

Solute atoms or molecules can only form a solution when they become evenly separated by bits of solvent. The first part of a lump of solute to dissolve is the outer surface. If you put a sugar cube in water and stir, you will see that the corners of the cube dissolve first. Bit by bit the cube turns into a rounded shape that gets smaller and smaller. The innermost molecules in the cube are the last to dissolve.

Solutes will dissolve more quickly if we break them into smaller pieces. For example, a ground-up sugar cube dissolves faster than a whole one. Breaking something into small pieces increases the total surface area exposed to other substances. Each sugar molecule is closer to the surface and can be pulled quickly away from the rest by the solvent.

This deer is about to lick a mineral block. The deer's saliva acts as a solvent. The outside surface of the block will dissolve first.

Experiment
Smaller and hotter

Problem: How can I make salt dissolve faster?

Hypothesis: Salt will dissolve more quickly in smaller pieces. It will also dissolve more quickly in warmer water.

You will need:
- table salt
- a stopwatch
- a teaspoon
- a pen and paper
- a scale balance
- six jam jars
- rock salt
- a cup

Procedure:
1. Weigh a teaspoon of rock salt and put it into a jar. Then, put the same weight of table salt in another jar.
2. Carefully pour a cup of hot tap water onto the table salt and stir. Using the stopwatch, time and record how long it takes to dissolve.
3. Repeat for the rock salt.
4. Repeat steps 1 and 2 using cold tap water.
5. Repeat steps 1 and 2 using ice water.

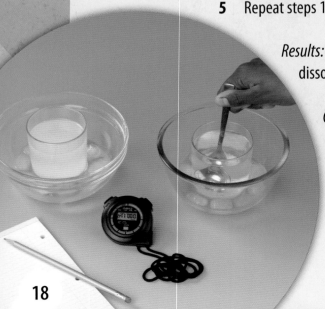

Results: Which combination of salt and water dissolved fastest?

Conclusion: Water molecules have more energy when they are hot, so they dissolve the salt faster. Table salt dissolves faster than rock salt because it has a larger surface area.

How Can We Separate Mixtures and Solutions?

In a mixture or **solution**, the different types of **matter** are mixed up. However, they have not combined to form new substances. Their **atoms** or **molecules** can be separated again. We use differences in **physical properties** between substances to separate them.

Settling down

The difference in weight and **density** of substances often allows them to separate into different layers. For example, shake up a cup of garden soil with water in a sealed jar and leave it to stand. After a few days, separate layers will form.

This soil mixture has settled. You can see the layers of different materials.

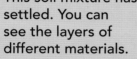

Did you know?
Mixtures in reverse

Some mixtures can be separated into substances identical to those originally mixed together. The **physical change** is **reversible**. However, other separations of mixtures are not truly reversible. For example, a smoothie can only be separated into distinct types of fruit pulp but not into complete fruits.

Sieving and filtering

A **sieve** can be used to separate parts of a mixture by size. It only allows matter below a certain size to get through. Sieves are used for many things, including draining pasta and catching fish.

Filters are very fine sieves that can separate small **particles** from each other. Paper and cloth can be filters. No filter can stop single molecules from getting through, but some are very fine. For example, ceramic filters in water treatment plants are used to trap tiny living things called bacteria in dirty water. The bacteria could make people sick if they drank them.

Magnetism

We can use the force of **magnetism** to separate some mixtures. For example, waste metals such as empty food and drink cans are taken past a powerful magnet. The magnet picks up anything made from magnetic metals, such as iron or steel.

Enormous magnets powered by electricity are used to separate steel objects from a mixture of other waste metals. They then carry the steel into trucks that take it away for recycling.

Demonstration
Metal food

We need to eat a small amount of iron in food to keep us healthy. Often it is found in tiny amounts in **compounds** we eat. However, it is also found in large bits mixed into some breakfast cereals!

You will need:

- bran cereal
- a wooden spoon
- plastic wrap
- a cup
- a magnet
- two helpers

Procedure:

1 Crush the bran cereal in the cup using one end of the wooden spoon. Grind it into the smallest pieces you can.
2 Get your helpers to hold and stretch a piece of plastic wrap out flat using both hands.
3 Carefully pour the cereal onto the plastic wrap.
4 Hold the magnet underneath the mixture, underneath the wrap.
5 Gently blow the mixture from one side. Is anything staying put immediately above the magnet?

Explanation:
Grinding and then magnetism separated this mixture. The little black bits remaining on the plastic wrap are iron filings attracted to the magnet.

Separating solutions

We can separate solutions by changing the **state** of either the **solvent** or the **solute**. When a **liquid** changes to a **gas**, it is called **evaporation**. Evaporation happens when atoms or molecules at the surface of a liquid move around very fast. They spread out so much that they become a gas or **vapor**. For example, our bodies produce a salt solution (sweat) when we are hot. Water molecules evaporate from sweat, leaving salt behind. The water gets its extra movement energy from heat or by being bashed by moving air molecules.

Did you know?
Making sea salt

Sometimes people make sea salt from seawater. Seawater is a solution of salt and water. Seawater is collected in flat ponds. The sun and wind evaporate the water. The flakes of salt crystals left behind are collected. They are packaged and then sold to people to flavor their food.

This worker is using a special rake to collect salt crystals from the water.

Capturing solvents

Condensation happens when a gas cools down and becomes a liquid. It is the opposite of evaporation. Condensation is the reason a cold mirror fogs up after you have taken a hot shower. Some of the hot water evaporated into the air as water vapor. Then, it condensed into liquid water as it hit the cold surface of the mirror.

We can use condensation to separate solutions. If you collect the vapor evaporating from a solution and then cool it down, it forms a liquid. This process is often called **distilling**. Distilled water is often used to make medicines. Water from taps or other sources contains **dissolved** substances that could make the medicines work differently. Distilling factories boil water in large containers with tubes coming from them. As the steam moves along the tubes, it condenses, and distilled water drips from the end.

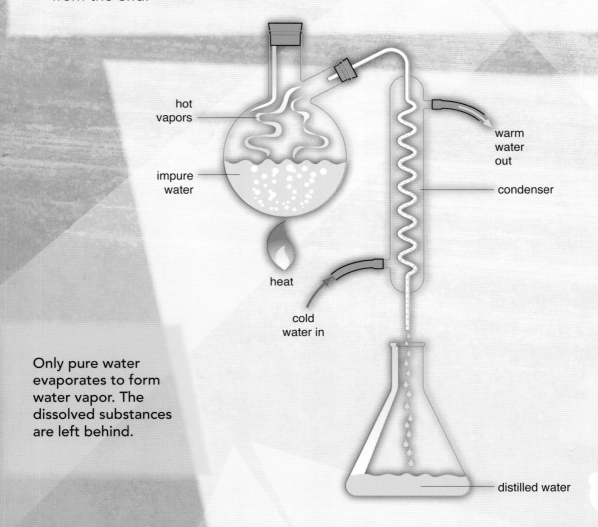

hot vapors

impure water

heat

warm water out

condenser

cold water in

distilled water

Only pure water evaporates to form water vapor. The dissolved substances are left behind.

Demonstration:
Multicolored black marker

The black ink in a nonpermanent marker is actually made up of a mixture of different colors. You can filter ink through paper towel to see the colors.

You will need:
- a nonpermanent black marker
- a piece of paper towel
- a saucer
- an eyedropper

Procedure:
1. Using the marker, draw a black spot in the middle of the paper towel.
2. Place the paper towel on the saucer. Use the dropper to put a few drops of water on the black spot.
3. Leave the paper towel for 10 minutes, then look at it again. How many different colored inks can you spot?

Explanation: The marker's ink contains different inks dissolved in water. This solution moves across the paper towel. The molecules in the different colored inks travel different distances depending on their size. They leave rings of different colors around the black spot.

What Are Some Common Solutions?

Many familiar **solutions** are made by people. For example, we mix water and chlorine to use as a cleaning substance in swimming pools. However, two of the most common solutions in the world occur naturally. They are seawater and **acid rain**.

Salt water

Two-thirds of Earth's surface is covered with one solution! Most oceans have very similar **concentrations** of salts. Water constantly evaporates from their vast surfaces, leaving salt behind. However, oceans do not usually get saltier. Freshwater from rivers and other sources keeps them topped off. Moving water in oceans keeps the solution mixed.

Some small seas in very hot places have very high salt concentrations. This is because there is more **evaporation** and little river water entering or leaving them. For example, the Dead Sea is ten times saltier than normal seawater.

It is easy to float in the Dead Sea! The dissolved salts make the water very **dense**.

Harmful rain

People burn fuels to create energy for heat. Burning fuels release **gas compounds** such as sulfur dioxide and nitrogen dioxide into the air. These gases can make the air dirty. Acids in the air mix with rainwater to form acid rain. The acid in this solution is as concentrated as the acid in lemon juice. Acid rain can damage leaves on trees and harm fish and frogs in ponds and lakes.

Did you know?
Creating caves

Carbon dioxide in small amounts is normal in the atmosphere. It forms weak acid rain. After it falls, some seeps underground. Over thousands of years, it can gradually **dissolve** soft rocks such as limestone. Sometimes this creates caves. Some of the dissolved rock made when caves form drains away. However, water evaporates from some, creating weird rock shapes.

Hanging stalactites and standing stalagmites are some of the new rock shapes made when caves form.

Demonstration
Make a stalagmite and stalactite

You will need:

- two jam jars
- salt
- a spoon
- a jam jar lid
- four 12-inch- (30-centimeter-) long pieces of yarn twisted together

Procedure:

1 Fill both jars with hot tap water. Spoon and stir enough salt into each jar to make **saturated** solutions (see pages 10 and 11).
2 Place the jars in a warm place with the lid on the ground between them. Dip the ends of the twisted yarn in the jars so the middle hangs over the lid.
3 After a few minutes the solution will run along the yarn and start to drip off the middle onto the lid. Leave this for a week. Then, measure your stalactites and stalagmites!

Explanation: Water evaporates from the solution dripping off the yarn. This leaves tiny crystals. Over time, the crystals join together, forming a large, hard drip off the yarn and one on the lid below.

WHAT IS AIR MADE FROM?

One of the most common mixtures on Earth is air. It is a mixture of different **gases**. The percentage of different gases in air remains almost the same wherever you are on Earth.

- Over three-quarters of the air is nitrogen. Tiny living things in soil take in nitrogen gas from the air. Plants take in some of this nitrogen, **dissolved** in water, through their roots and use it to remain healthy.

- Nearly a quarter of air is made up of oxygen. Most animals, including people, need oxygen to survive. This gas is essential in producing energy from food so we can live and grow.

- The rest of air is made up of small amounts of other gases, including carbon dioxide and water **vapor**.

This pie chart shows the percentages of different gases making up air.

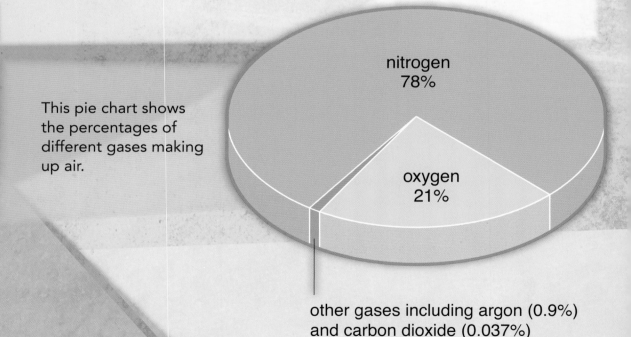

nitrogen
78%

oxygen
21%

other gases including argon (0.9%) and carbon dioxide (0.037%)

Ways of breathing

- Many animals breathe in air to get the oxygen they need. Oxygen is carried around our bodies from our lungs after it dissolves in the blood. Some animals that live underwater, including whales, have to come to the surface regularly to breathe.

- Others, such as diving beetles, carry a bubble of air underwater with them, similar to the way human divers carry air in tanks on their backs. However, deep-sea divers' tanks carry air with a lower **concentration** of nitrogen than normal air. The **pressure** is greater in water than out of it and it increases with depth. As divers go deeper, more nitrogen dissolves in their blood than normally would. This is because gas **solubility** increases. Nitrogen can form bubbles in bodies if divers rise to the surface too quickly. These bubbles can make divers very sick. Breathing the right mix of gas keeps divers safe.

- Most underwater animals, including fish and lobsters, get the oxygen they need from the water around them. They have special structures called gills that separate the dissolved oxygen from the water.

Divers breathe in oxygen from air in their tanks. The bubbles coming from this diver are carbon dioxide gas he has breathed out.

Glossary

acid rain rainwater containing harmful, dissolved gases

atom one of the tiny particles that make up matter

chemical property describes how a substance behaves when combined with other substances

compound formed from two or more substances

concentration amount of a substance in a given volume of solution

condensation change of state from gas to liquid

density amount of a substance in a certain volume

diluted make a solution weaker by increasing the proportion of solvent

dissolve when solute breaks down and spreads out in a solvent

distill evaporate solvent from a solution and condense the gas into a liquid again

evaporation change of state from liquid to gas

gas state of matter in which atoms or molecules are furthest apart

insoluble cannot dissolve

liquid state of matter in which atoms or molecules are weakly held together with a definite volume but variable shape

magnetism force that causes some metals to move together or apart

mass amount or weight of matter

matter anything with weight that takes up space

molecule two or more atoms joined together

particle very small piece of material

physical change change in a physical property, such as dissolving

physical property characteristic of a substance, such as its state or hardness

pressure force against the surface area of a substance

reversible change that can go backward or forward

saturated when a solution can dissolve no more solute

sieve device that can physically separate parts of a mixture by size

solid state of matter in which atoms or molecules are packed tightly together in a definite shape

solubility how much of a solute can dissolve in a particular volume of solvent

solute substance that dissolves

solution mixture made when one substance dissolves in another

solvent substance that the solute dissolves in

state form of matter—solid, liquid, or gas

suspension mixture containing small pieces of insoluble substance

vapor gas

vibrate shake around on the spot

volume space that something takes up

Further Resources

Books

Baldwin, Carol. *Mixtures, Compounds, and Solutions* (*Freestyle Express: Material Matters* series). Chicago: Raintree, 2006.

Ballard, Carol. *Solids, Liquids, and Gases* (*Science Answers* series). Chicago: Heinemann Library, 2004.

Nankivell-Aston, Sally, and Dorothy Jackson. *Water* (*Science Experiments* series). New York: Franklin Watts, 2000.

Riley, Peter. *Magnetism* (*Straightforward Science* series). New York: Franklin Watts, 1999.

Websites

Find out more about mixtures and test your knowledge with a quiz at:
www.chem4kids.com/files/matter_mixture.html

Make your own crystals from saturated solutions at:
www.bbc.co.uk/schools/podsmission/solidsandliquids/

Learn more about mixures at:
http://www.cartage.org.lb/en/kids/science/Chemistry/Matter/Mixtures.htm

Index